COPYRIGHTS

First published in Great Britain in **2023** by BWF publishing

© Book Writing Founders Publishing UK, **2023**

Text copyright © Sety H., **2023**

Cover illustration and design, and decorative inside art © Book Writing Founders UK

Full-page inside illustrations by BWF,

The moral rights of the author has been asserted

All characters and events in this publication other than those in the public domain, are fictitious and any resemblance to real persons, living or dead is purely coincidental. All rights reserved

No part of this publication maybe reproduced, stored in a retrieval system or transmitted in any form or by any means, without the prior permission in writing of the publisher, nor be otherwise circulated in any form of binding or cover other than that in which it is published and without a similar condition including this condition being imposed on the subsequent purchaser.

ISBN: **9781962380423**
Book writing founders publishing
86-90 Paul Street, London EC2A 4NE

https://www.bookwritingfounders.co.uk

Our books may be purchased in bulk for promotional, educational, or business use.
Please contact Book writing founders at **+44-203-885-5296**, or by email at mailto:info@bookwritingfounders.co.uk.

First Edition **2023**

Dedication

To my boys. I am so proud of you.
To all readers, young and not so young, who will open this book. Never forget your inner child, it can often guide you and remind you of the joy in the little things.

Acknowledgements

To the friends that gave me the courage, the professionals who brought it into the world, and to my husband who always believed in me. Thank you.

BObby
and the
Magical Rainbow

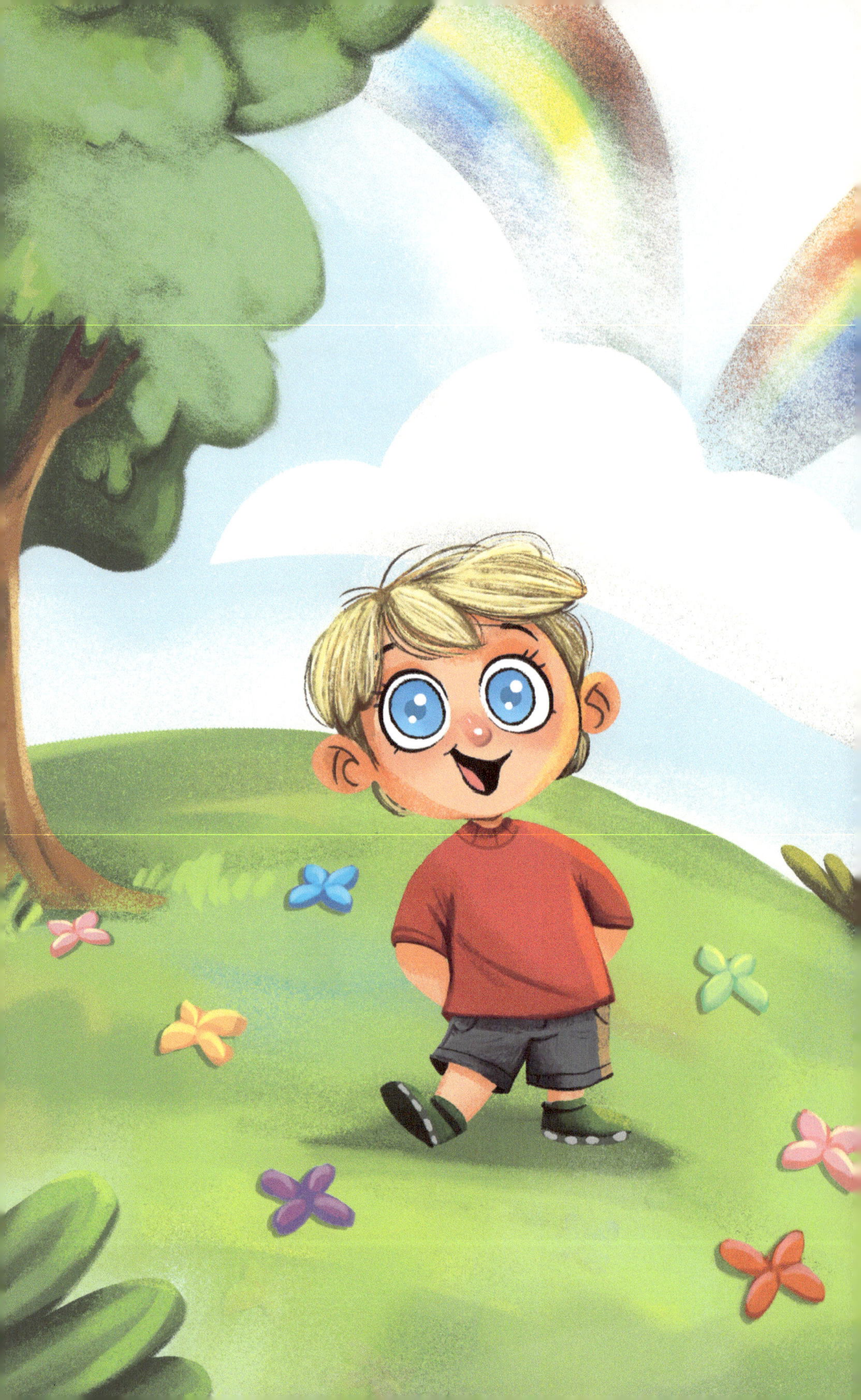

Once upon a time, there was a land where beautiful, colourful rainbows appeared in the sky every day. In this vibrant land lived little Bobby and his family. Bobby was a very playful boy, and like any child, he loved to run, jump, and play with his friends.

One day, Kaya came to ask Bobby to go out to the meadow in front of Bobby's little house and play hide-and-seek. However, Bobby wanted to play tag. Both wanted to play a lot, but neither wanted to give in to what the other wanted.

Bobby got very annoyed, and in his anger, he yelled at Kaya that he didn't want to play with her anymore and pushed her aside. Kaya looked at him angrily, and with clenched fists, she said:
"I don't want to be friends anymore!"
Kaya spun around and ran home, leaving Bobby alone in the meadow.

The anger that Bobby had felt just a moment ago seemed to evaporate, and suddenly he felt sad, lonely, and tired. He sat down on the green grass and started to cry.

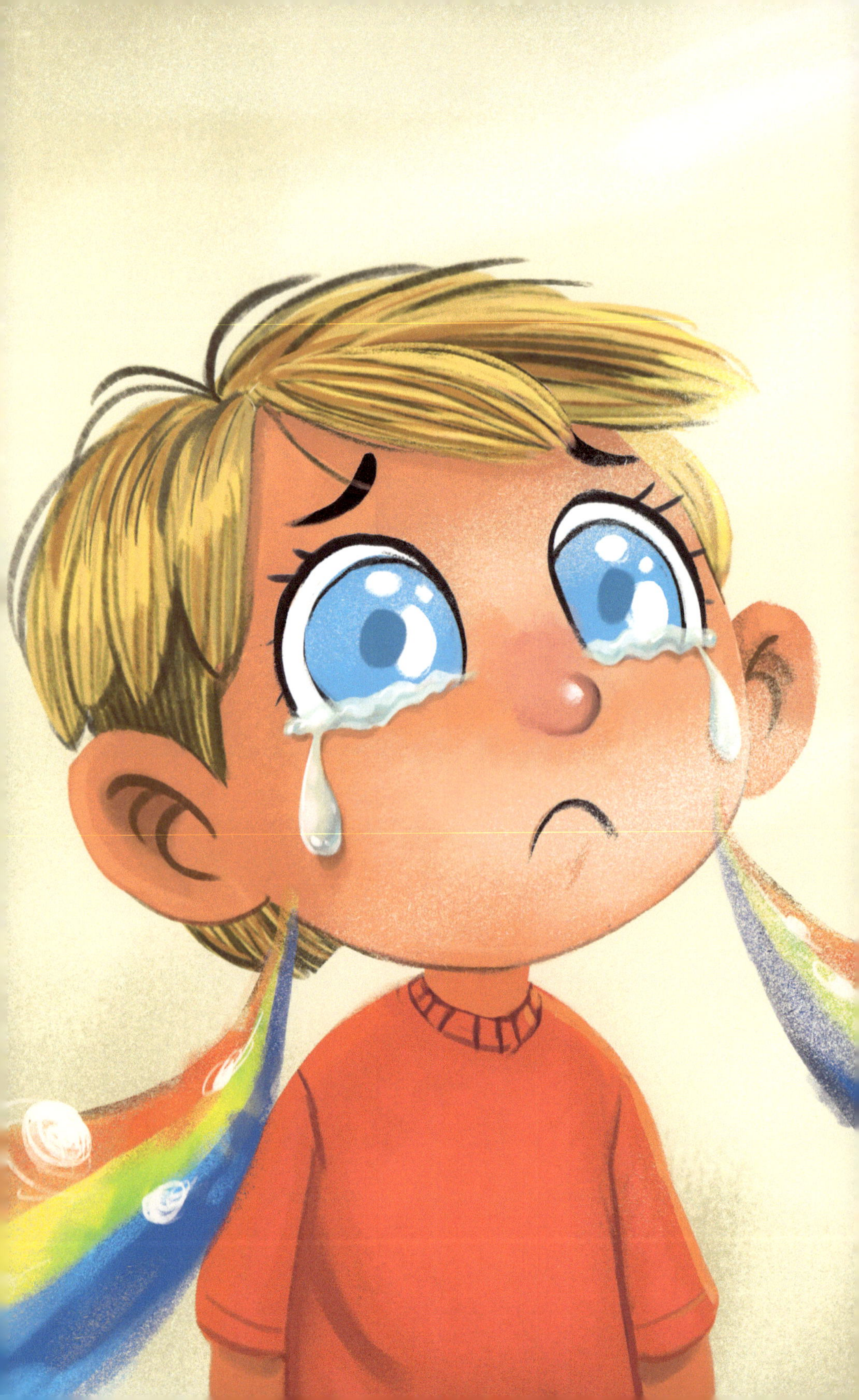

Big tears rolled down his cheeks. A ray of sunshine illuminated one of his tears, and a huge RAINBOW appeared from that teardrop. Bobby jumped back in surprise and exclaimed: "Wow! What a beautiful rainbow! Where did it come from?"

"Hello, Bobby! I am the Rainbow where your emotions and values live. I am a part of you!" said the Rainbow, and its colours shimmered even brighter. Bobby couldn't believe his eyes. He had never seen such a rainbow before. Where had it come from, and why now? Bobby had so many questions.

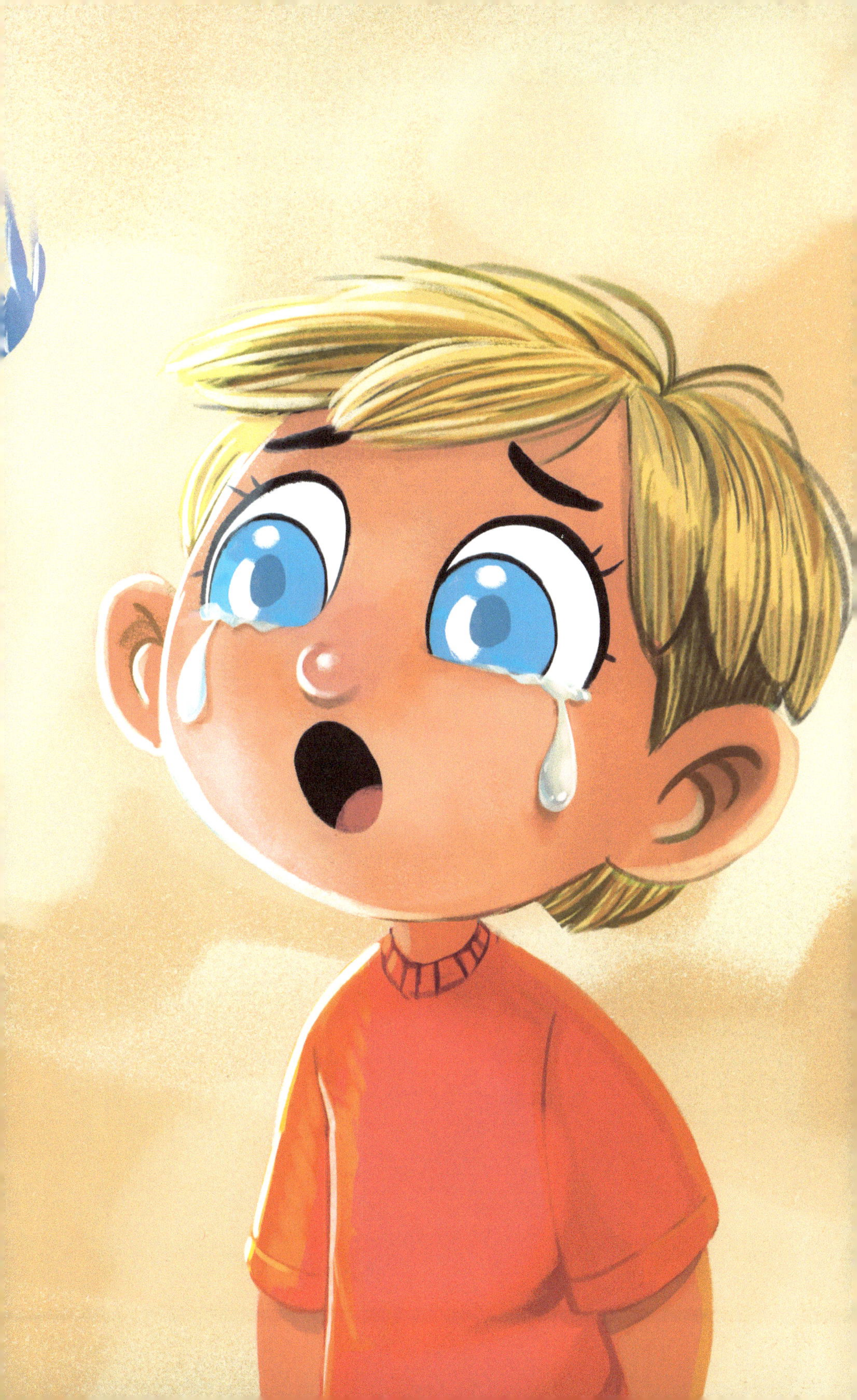

"I didn't know that someone lived in the Rainbow. I didn't know there was a Rainbow inside of me! And what are VALUES?" asked Bobby, still in disbelief. "Are they some sort of special fish?"

"What a wonderful question, Bobby," the Rainbow chimed. "Values are little miracles that we all have, and with them, we make the world MORE BEAUTIFUL AND KIND." The Rainbow continued, "I am here because I sensed how upset you were and needed to help you. You see, each of my colours represents a different emotion and value, and they are here to help you understand them and find the right path."

At that moment, the red colour of the Rainbow shimmered and started bouncing lightly. Bobby watched with wide-open eyes. He couldn't believe it.

Then he heard the voice of the Rainbow again, saying, "Come, Bobby. See what Red wants to show you!" Bobby took a step forward, and the red colour of the Rainbow sparkled even brighter, transforming into a red road. Bobby took another step forward, and another, and another. Red was all around him, so **beautiful**.

Suddenly, a little red troll with funny, long, red hair appeared before him, wearing glasses on its head and a gentle smile.

"Hello, Bobby," the troll said. "I've been waiting for us to meet. I am the Red Troll of Respect—Reddy."

"Hello," Bobby said in astonishment. "How do you know my name?"

"I am a part of you. I live in the Rainbow in your mind, just like all the other colourful trolls of the Rainbow," Reddy explained. The Red Troll extended its hand, and Bobby reached out in return. "Nice to meet you."

"Nice to meet you too," Bobby replied. "SO, WHAT IS RESPECT?"

Reddy clapped its hands and explained, "Respect is when we treat others well, listen to them, help them, and keep our promises. Respect is also found in our daily little things, like greeting people.

Do you remember yesterday when you and your mom walked in the park and passed by a kind gentleman? He didn't know you but smiled and said, 'Good day.' Your mom replied with the same greeting. That's Respect for others."

"Or when you're playing with a friend, but both of you want to play different things—you can make a plan together. First, play one thing, then the other. That way, you respect each other's wishes."

Bobby's cheeks flushed red as he remembered what he had done to Kaya. He hadn't shown her Respect! He hadn't listened to her wishes and had treated her rudely. He hung his head low, and tears welled up in his eyes once again.

Then the troll said, "Bobby, dear child, don't be sad. We all make mistakes. When you see Kaya, just hug her and tell her how you feel. I'm sure she will forgive you. True friends respect each other and forgive each other."

Bobby sniffled and smiled faintly with hope. "Thank you! That's exactly what I'll do!"

"An excellent decision. Remember, when you respect the people around you, they will respect you back. When you're unsure or feeling sad, just close your eyes and think of the red colour of the Rainbow, where I live, and I will appear! Now go. Many paths are waiting for you."

Bobby clapped his hands, thanked Reddy, and set off, but not before giving the troll a goodbye hug.

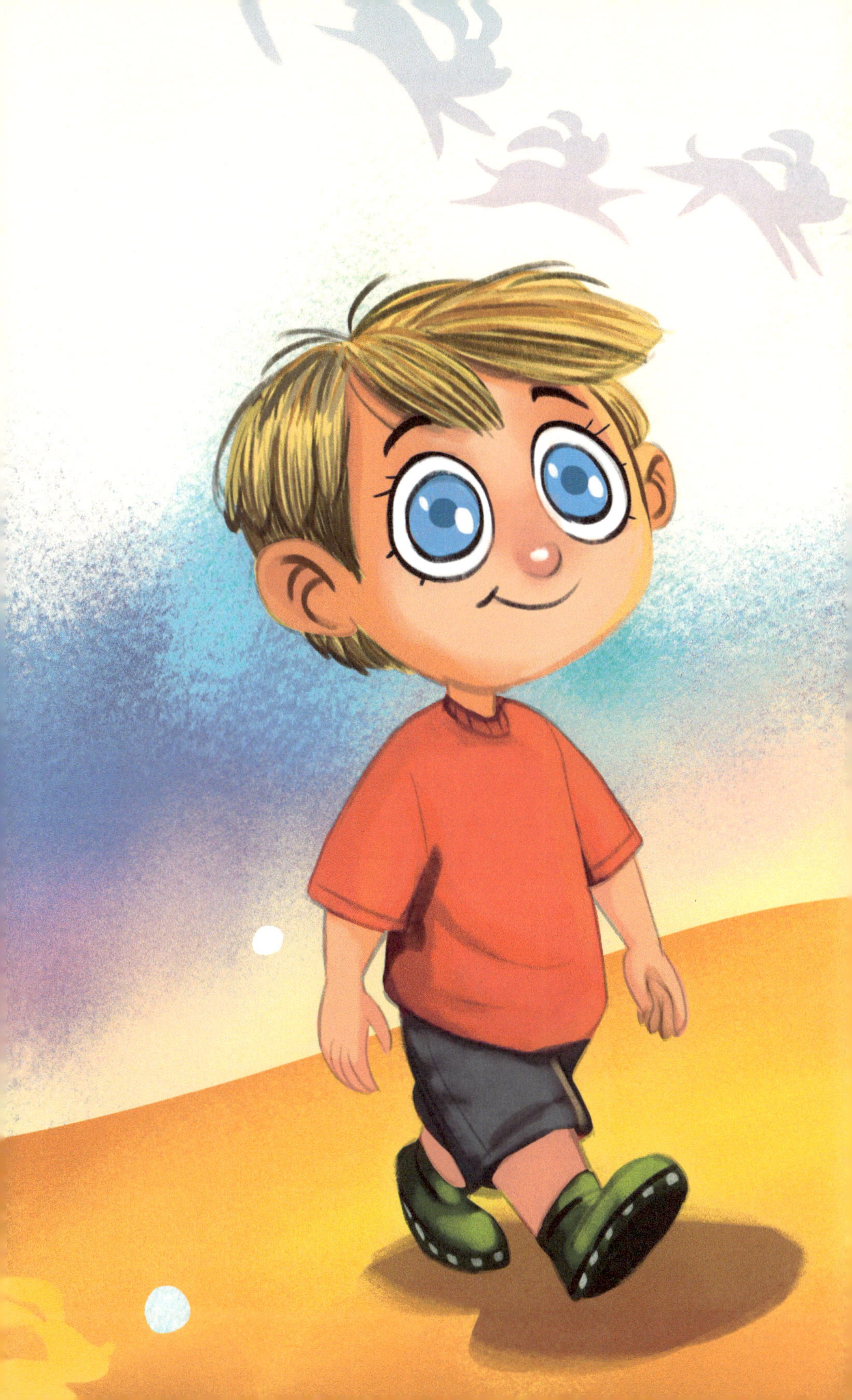

He took just a few steps, and everything around him turned orange. He had reached the orange road of the Rainbow. And as you can guess, before long, he saw a little orange troll trying to get an apple from a tree but couldn't quite reach it. The troll had the craziest hair you've ever seen, like a basket struck by lightning that now stood in all directions. But at the same time, it suited the troll perfectly.

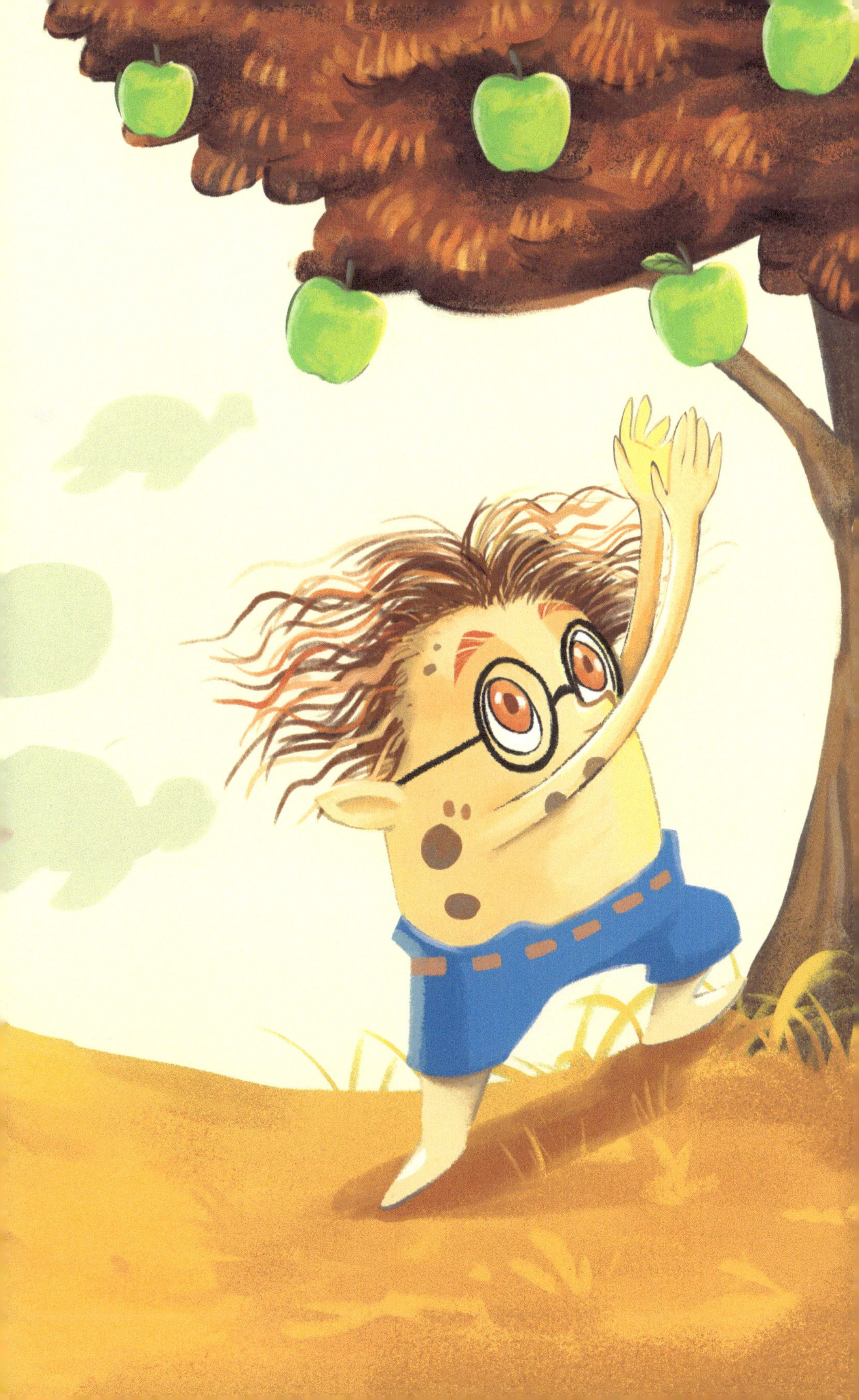

Bobby approached it confidently, waved, and kindly offered, "Hello! Can I help you with that apple?"

The orange troll turned towards Bobby with a huge smile on his tiny face. This troll had the sweetest eyes you could imagine.

"Thank you, Bobby. You are very kind!" - said the little troll.

"You're welcome. I'm happy to help," Bobby replied, lifted himself onto his tiptoes, and plucked a large apple. "What's your name?" he asked as he handed the apple to the troll.

"You can call me Orie. I am the troll of Kindness."
"Do you also live in my head, like the Red Troll?" Bobby continued.

"Yes! Exactly. But it seems that you already know very well what Kindness is. It's the most beautiful and warm feeling. Like when you help others. Just like you helped me now. Or, for example, when you apologize to Kaya for pushing her. That's Kindness too."

Bobby knew well what he needed to do and quickly wished the troll a good day to continue on his path, find Kaya, and apologize to her.
He waved to Orie, who smiled back and said over his shoulder:

"You know where to find me if you need me! Bye, Bobby."

Bobby ran until he saw a beautiful green meadow beneath his feet. He stopped and looked around. He had found the green road of the Rainbow.

Sitting next to a green bush on a small green stool was a green troll with a green hat and strangely big feet. Such a curious creature with such big feet, Bobby thought.

"Hello!" they greeted each other.

"Welcome to the Green Road of **Honesty**. I am Greeny."

"It's very beautiful here," Bobby replied and introduced himself. "I love playing in the forest, among the trees and grass."

"Me too," the troll chimed happily. "You know what I love the most?" the troll continued.

"When people are honest with each other. Especially with their mom, dad, grandma, grandpa, and friends. Do you know what it means to be honest?"

"Hmm, I think I do. But I'm not entirely sure. Actually, no, I don't know. Does it mean you love the forest?" Bobby guessed.

Greeny clapped its hands happily and smiled. "Mmm, not quite. But to be honest, means to tell the truth, just like you did when you said you didn't know. When we don't lie, we are being honest!"

"Ahh," Bobby continued. "My mom often tells me that it's not good to lie. And when we say the truth, we can always find a solution."

"Your mother, Bobby, is very wise. That's exactly it."

"Greeny, I like it here, but I need to find Kaya quickly and apologize for what I did. I'll come back, I promise!"

"Good luck, Bobby. I'll be here to remind you not to be afraid of the truth when you need it. Goodbye!"

"Goodbye," Bobby called out and continued on his way.

Bobby couldn't wait to see the next colour and meet his new friend. He wondered who it would be when everything around him turned blue like the sky on a sunny day.

Bobby slowed down and began looking around for the troll from the blue road of the Rainbow. Then he heard a voice and turned around towards it.

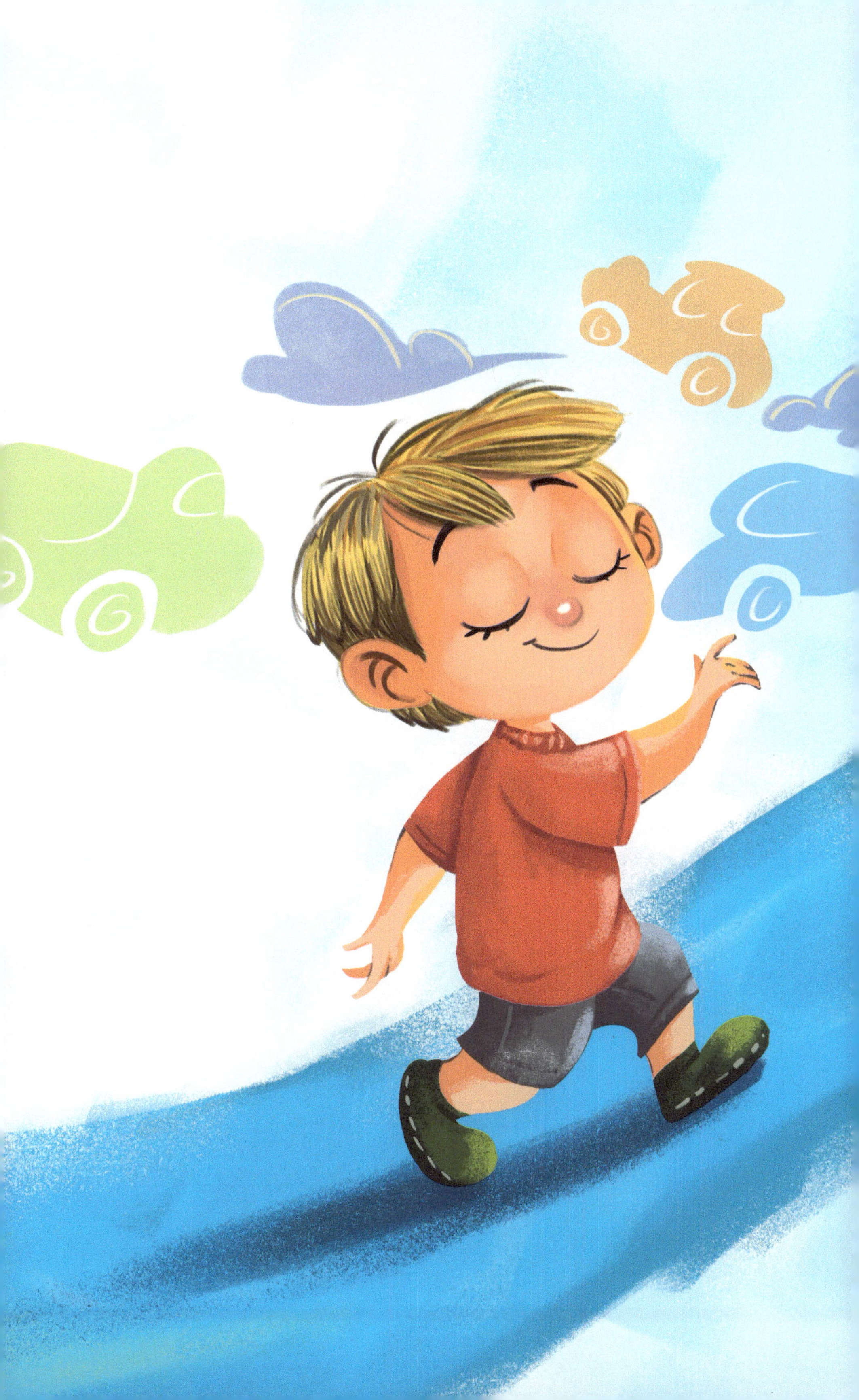

There, standing on a blue carpet, was the blue troll. He had a very long tail. Maybe its name was Bluey, Bobby thought. The troll was stacking blue cubes, and just as it reached the top of the cube tower, it collapsed and fell. The blue troll jumped up, clenched its fists, and Bobby thought it was about to burst in anger.

But the blue troll closed its eyes, **took a deep breath, exhaled loudly, and JUMPED TWICE.** How strange, Bobby thought to himself and asked, "Excuse me, are you okay?"

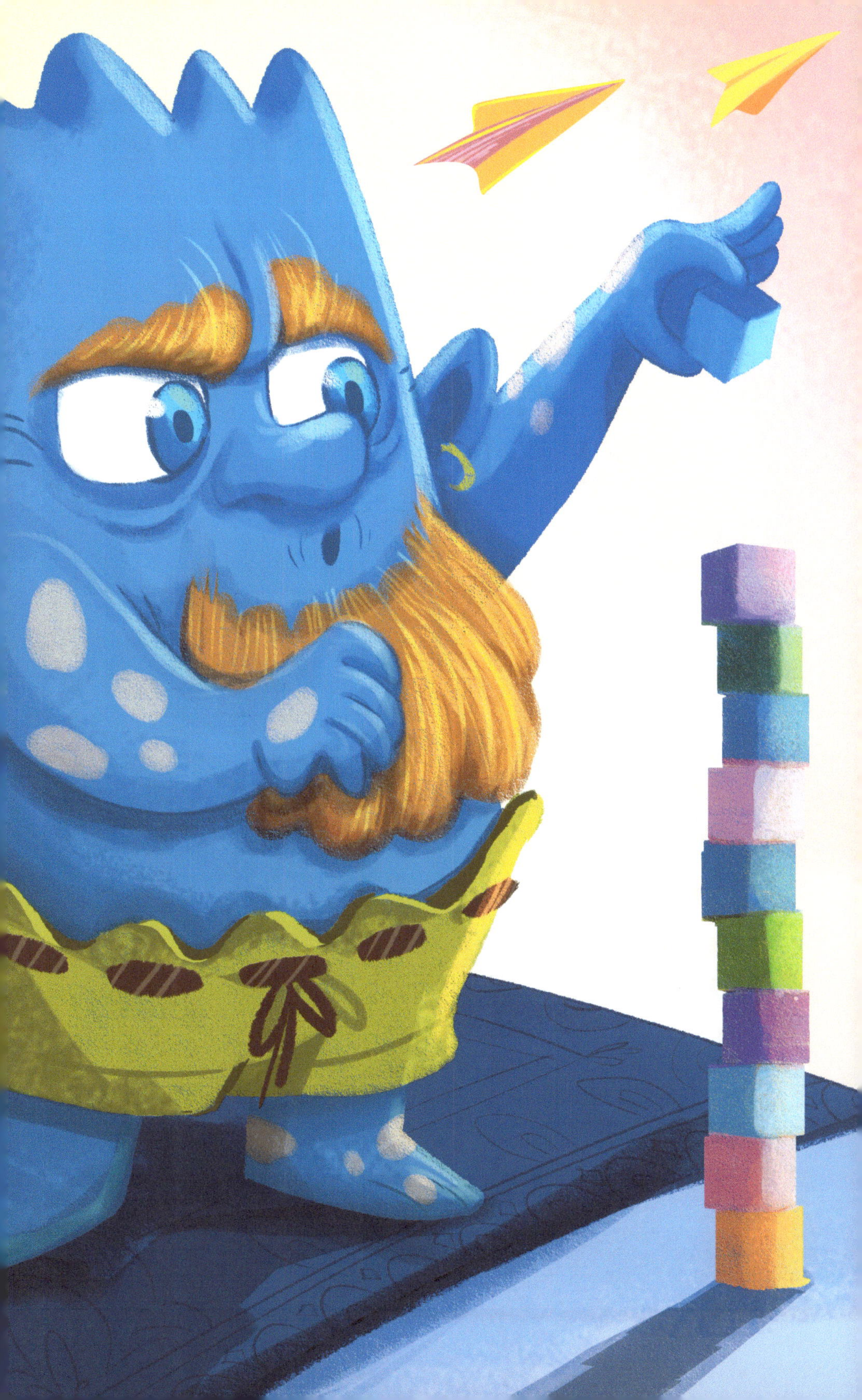

The blue troll turned towards Bobby and quickly smiled. "Bobby, my friend, hello," it said, opening its arms wide for a hug. "I've been waiting for you to meet me."

"Oh, really?" Bobby blinked, feeling confused. "I didn't know," he continued.

"Yes, whenever you get angry, I wait for you to see me. I am the troll of **Self-Control.** Self-control helps you calm down when you're angry, for example."

"Oh," Bobby simply said and felt a bit embarrassed. "Was that what you were doing just now when you got angry? Were you practicing self-control?" he asked uncertainly.

"Haha, yes, I was regulating my emotions. **We all get angry,** but there's no need to shout, hit, or... push."

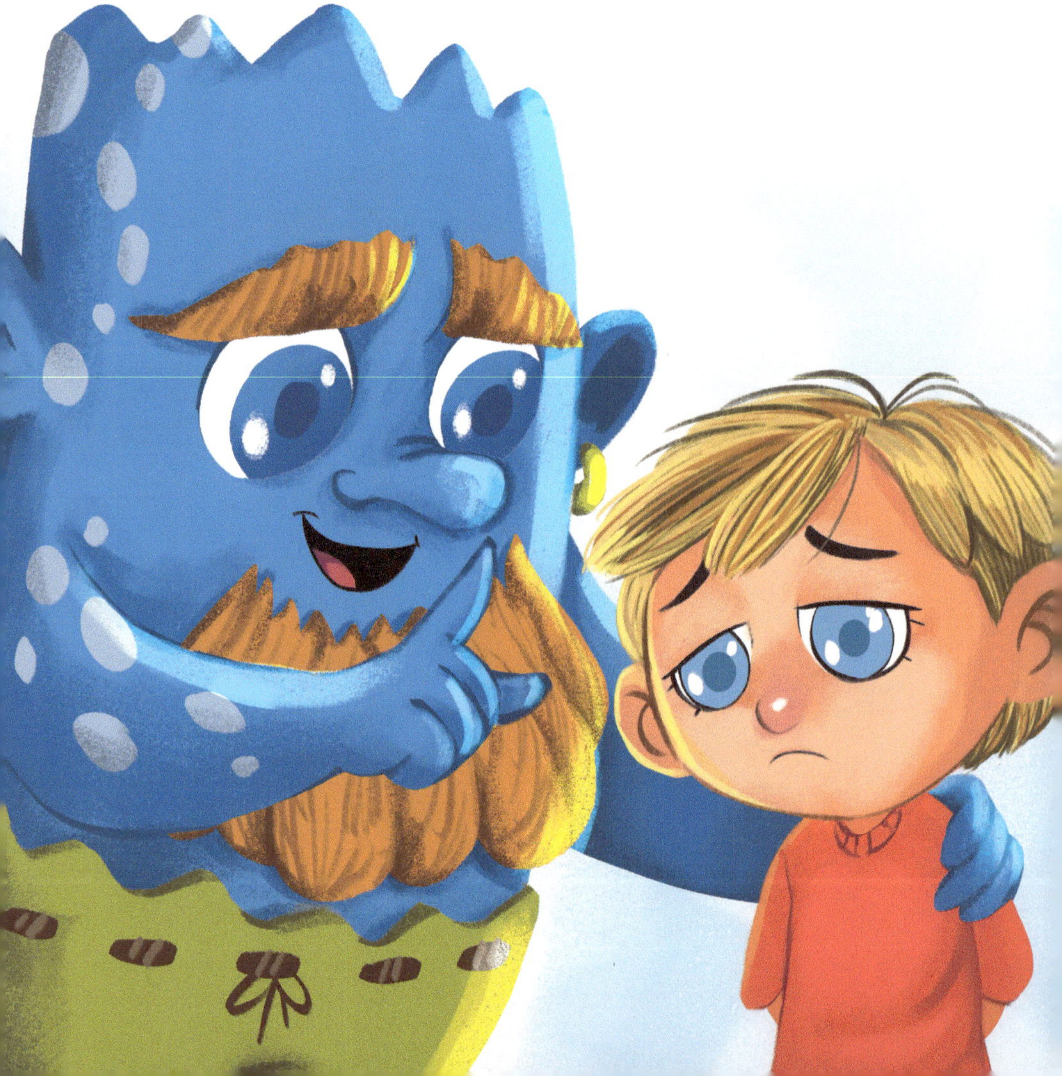

Bobby looked up with guilt written on his little face.

"Yes, Bobby, I was with you this morning when you pushed Kaya. But don't worry. I'm here to help you when you're angry, mad, upset, disappointed, or very sad. I'm always here, so don't forget. **JUST BREATHE.** You can also jump - it's really hard to be angry and jump at the same time. The important thing is to apologize and try to..."

"Control myself!", Bobby finished the sentence.
"Yes! You see, you know what to do. But it's a bit challenging to think when we're angry."
"Yeah," Bobby repeated thoughtfully. "It's **really hard for me to think when I'm so angry.**"

The blue troll hugged the determined Bobby tightly. "Remember, hugs help a lot when we're angry," the blue troll winked and let go of its embrace.

"Thank you, I'll remember! I promise!" said Bobby.
"I think you were in a hurry somewhere," the troll said. "But don't worry, I'm here when you need me."
"Yes! I need to find Kaya quickly and hug her so she won't be too mad at me!"
Bobby was about to leave when he remembered, "Oh, I forgot to ask! What's your name?"
"What's my name?" the blue troll chuckled.
"Well, it's TOD, of course!"
"TOD!" Bobby repeated, surprised and thought to himself that was really unexpected. "Bye, Tod!" Bobby gave him a high five and dashed down the blue road.

Suddenly he saw the most beautiful shade of purple. It was deep and rich. The path was filled with small dark purple flowers. Thousands and thousands of tiny blossoms.

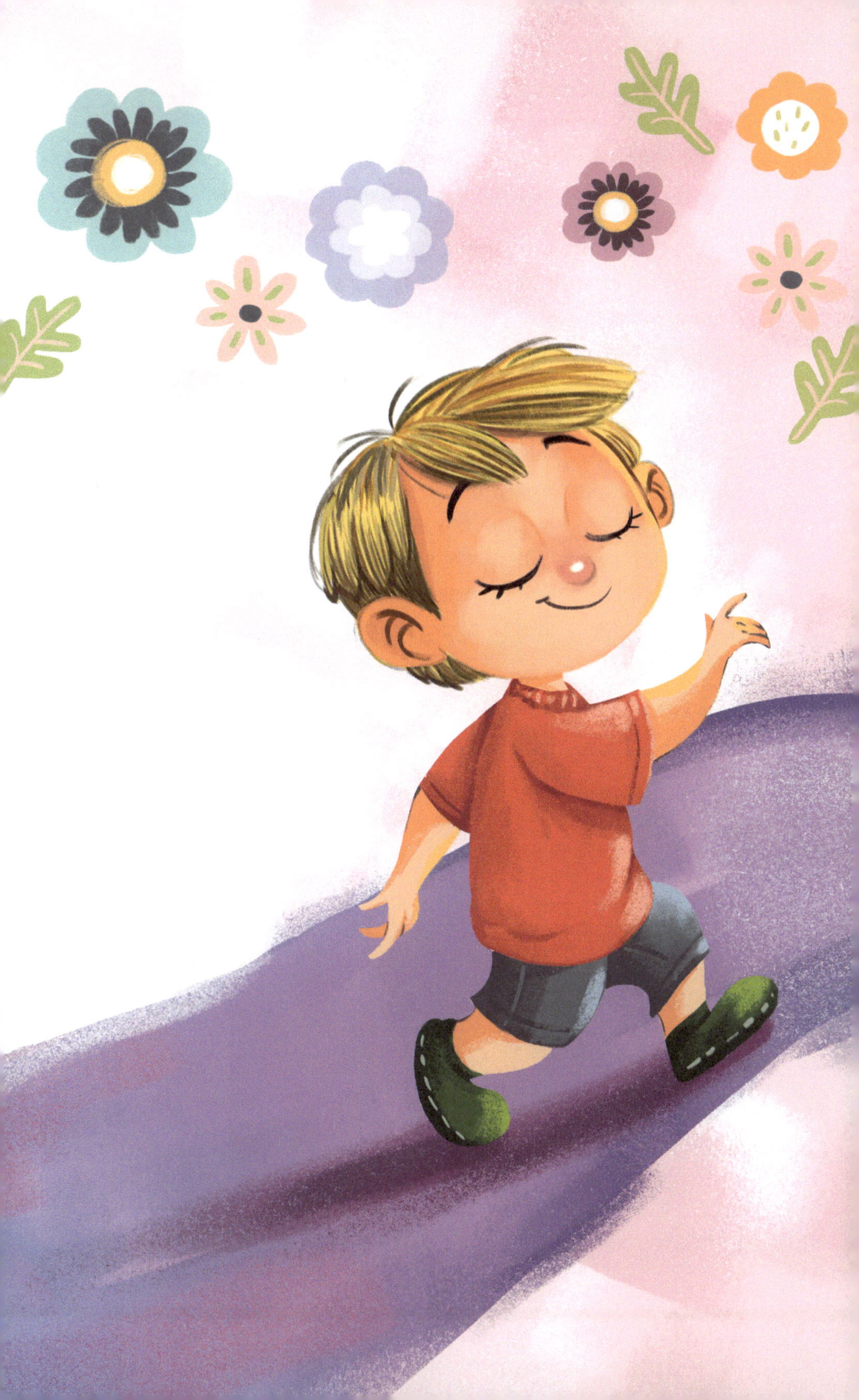

As Bobby admired the flowers, a purple troll suddenly jumped out and hugged him tightly.
"Oh, hello," Bobby said, patting the troll's long purple hair which was almost touching the ground.

The troll embraced Bobby and patted his back, saying: "Bobby, everything will be okay. I saw how upset you were today. First angry and then very sad. I understand you!" The troll continued to speak and comfort Bobby until he truly felt better. It was so **wonderful when someone understood you.** Just like Mom, Bobby thought to himself. The purple troll noticed that Bobby was feeling better and then introduced itself with a sweet smile: "Bobby, I'm Lily - the **Purple Troll of Empathy.** You can think of me whenever someone is sad, and you feel like hugging them to make them feel better. Or when someone is happy, and you feel happy for them."

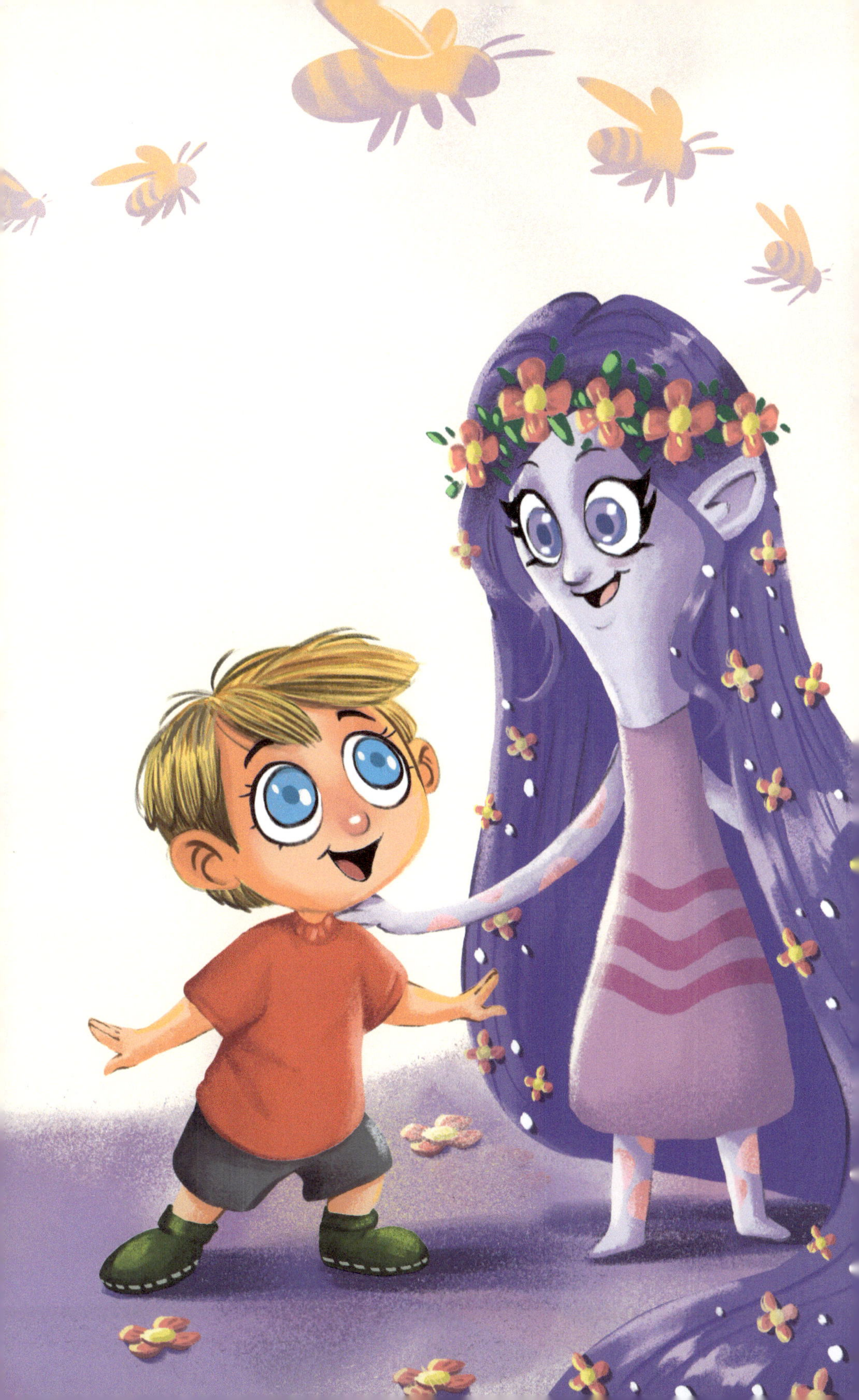

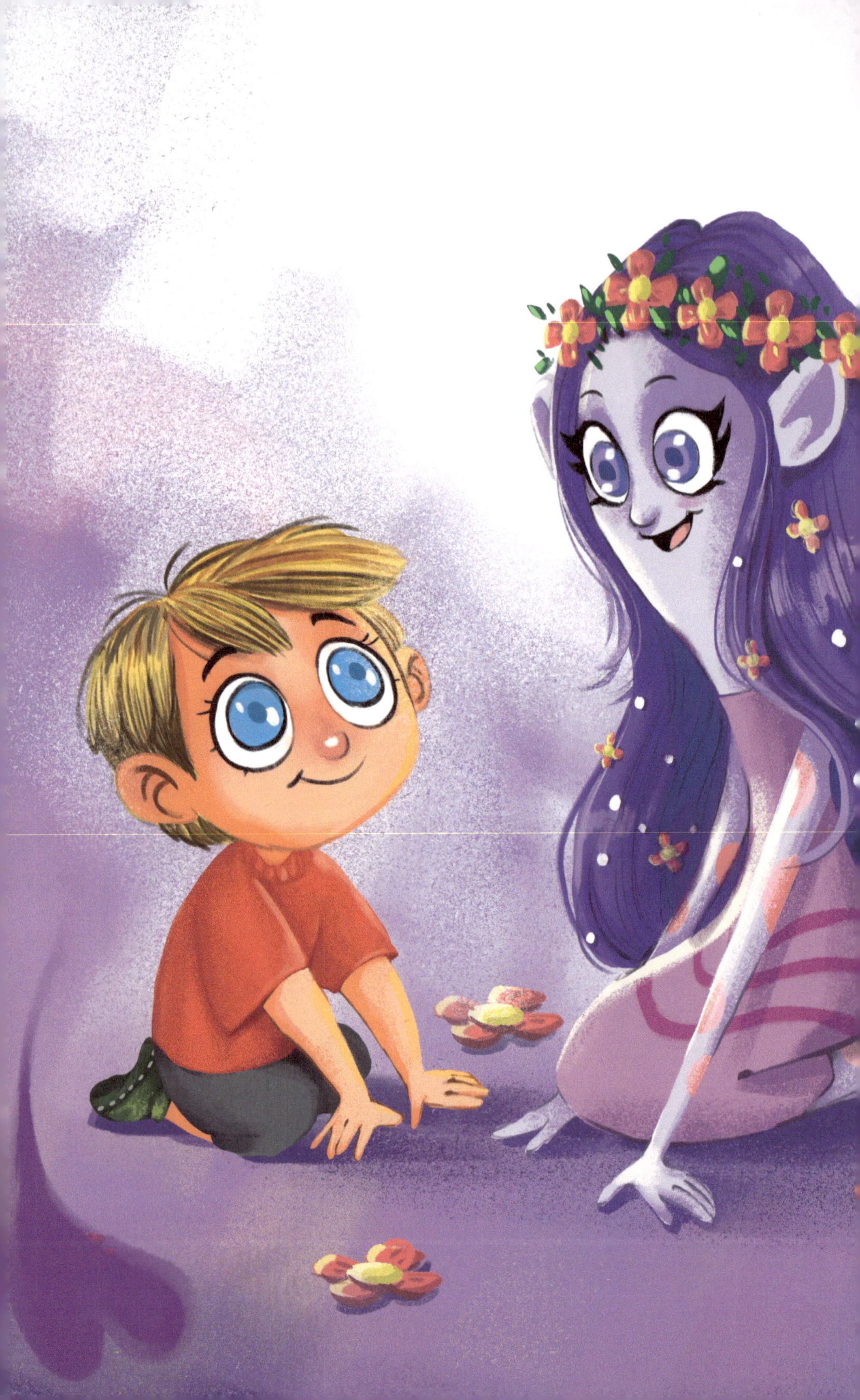

"I understand," said Bobby wisely. "Sometimes, Mom even cries when I cry. She empathizes with me very strongly!"

"Yes! Exactly! And now, are you ready for the last colour of the Rainbow?" Lily asked. "Yes," said Bobby, happily and genuinely calm. "Yes!" he repeated excitedly. He was about to go to Kaya, and everything would be fine again, and Bobby would have his friend back. "We'll meet again, Bobby. **Don't forget all emotions are normal. Understand and listen to your friends. That's how games are always more fun. And if someone does get angry: talk, hug each other, and forgive. We all get angry sometimes. Sometimes we just need a little time, and everything is okay again.**" "Thank you," Bobby said sincerely. "I won't forget." And Bobby hugged Lily once again because **we can always use one more hug. They are never enough.**

Bobby walked with a smile towards the last colour of the Rainbow, the pink colour.

He stepped into the beautiful pink shade, thinking another cheerful and rosy troll awaited him. But, oh, what a surprise. It was not like that at all.

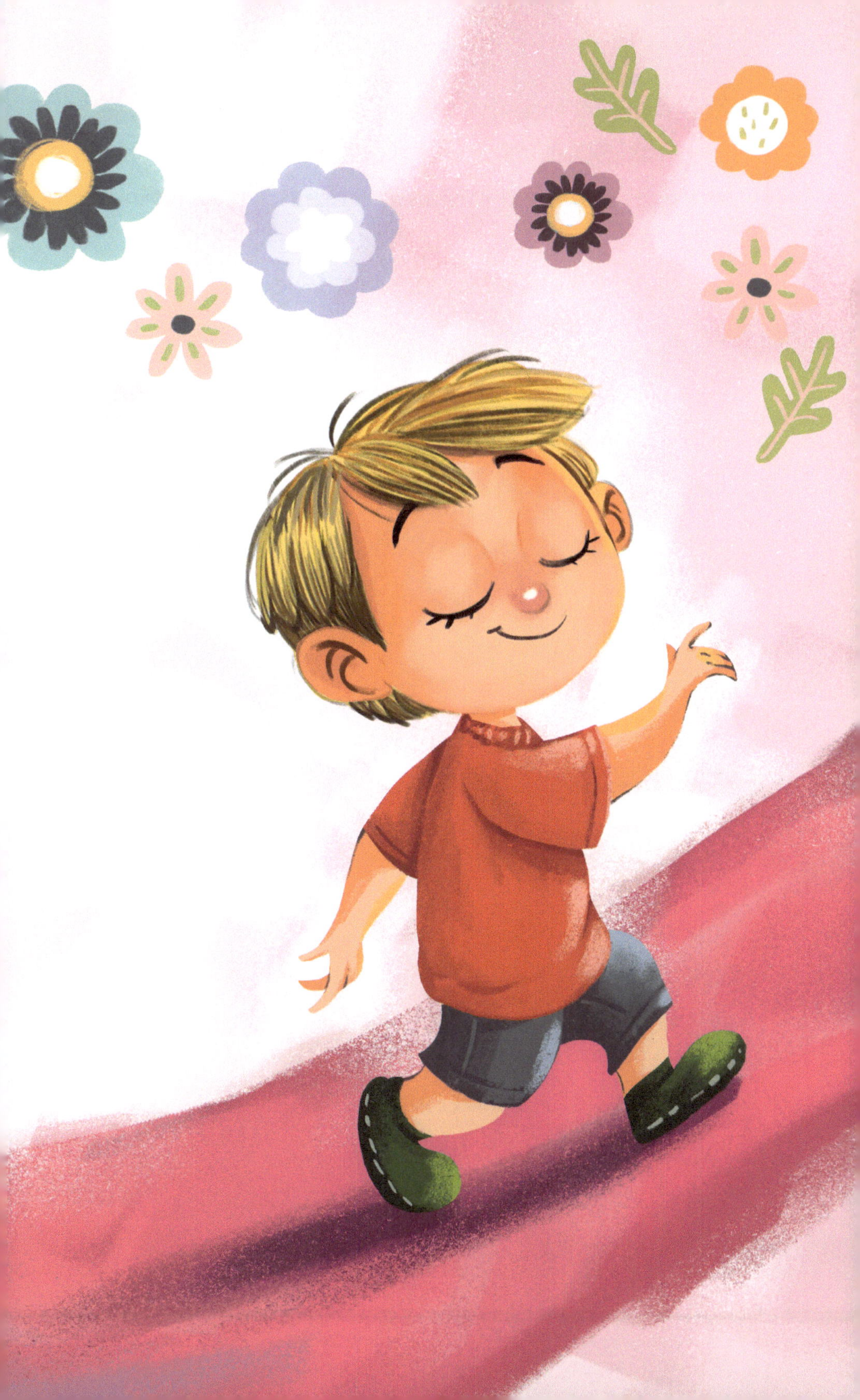

There, sitting together, were Reddy, Orie, Greeny, Lily, and TOD. They were all seated on a picnic blanket, indulging in sweet treats and laughing joyously, the five little trolls of the Rainbow. Respect, Kindness, Honesty, Empathy, and Self-Control - our values.

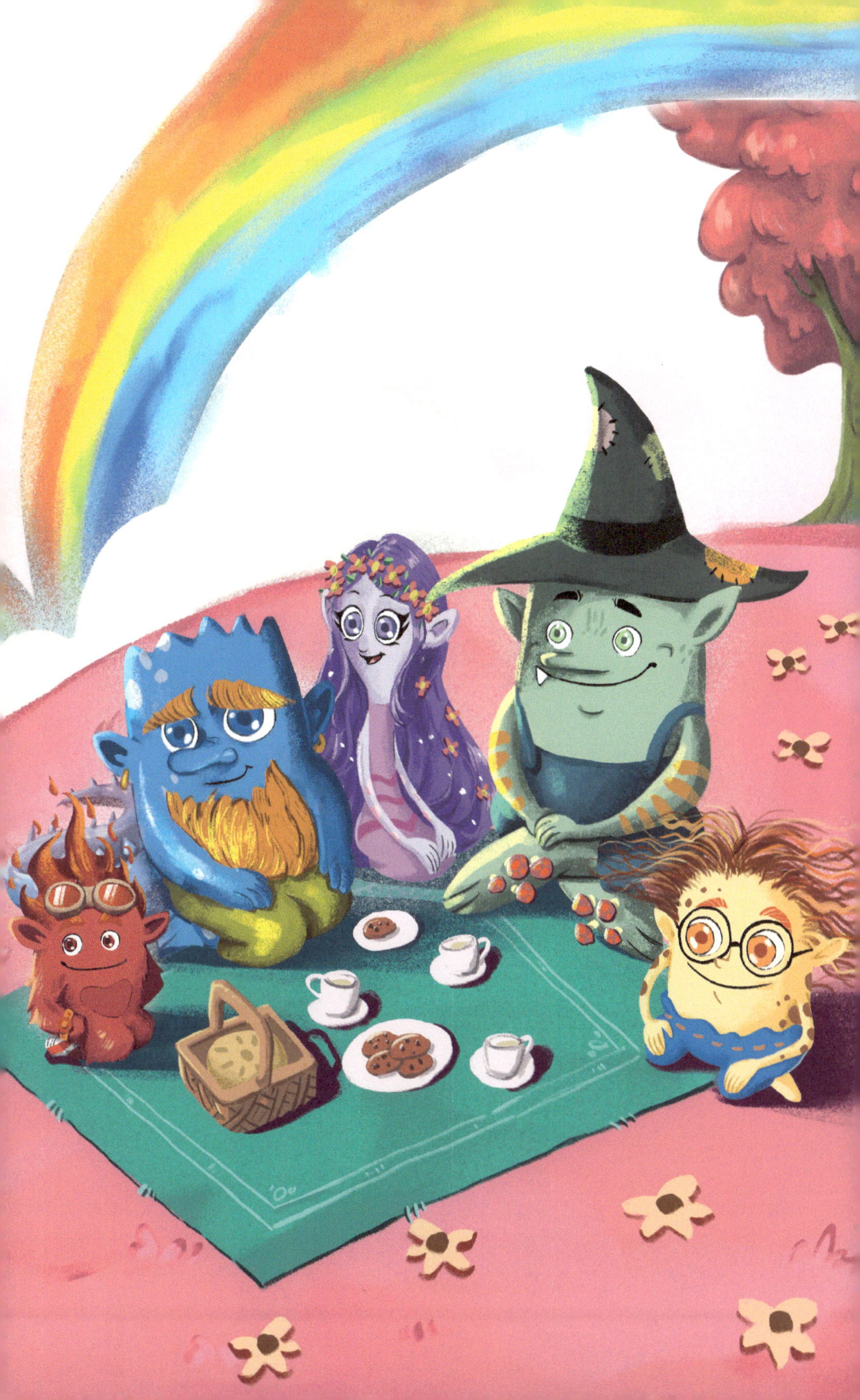

Bobby rushed towards them, shouting, "Hello, everyone!"
"Hello, Bobby!" they all shouted back as one.
"Welcome to the Pink Road- the colour of GRATITUDE."
"Well, isn't there..." Bobby began, but at that moment, the five trolls exchanged mischievous glances and moved aside, revealing the pink troll behind them.

"Don't think there's no pink troll on the Pink Road," the smiling troll said. "I am Rosy!" - The troll extended a hand to Bobby, revealing two delicate, white wings on its back.

"We love gathering together here every day for dinner and sharing stories about your adventures from the past day," explained Orie, the troll of Kindness.

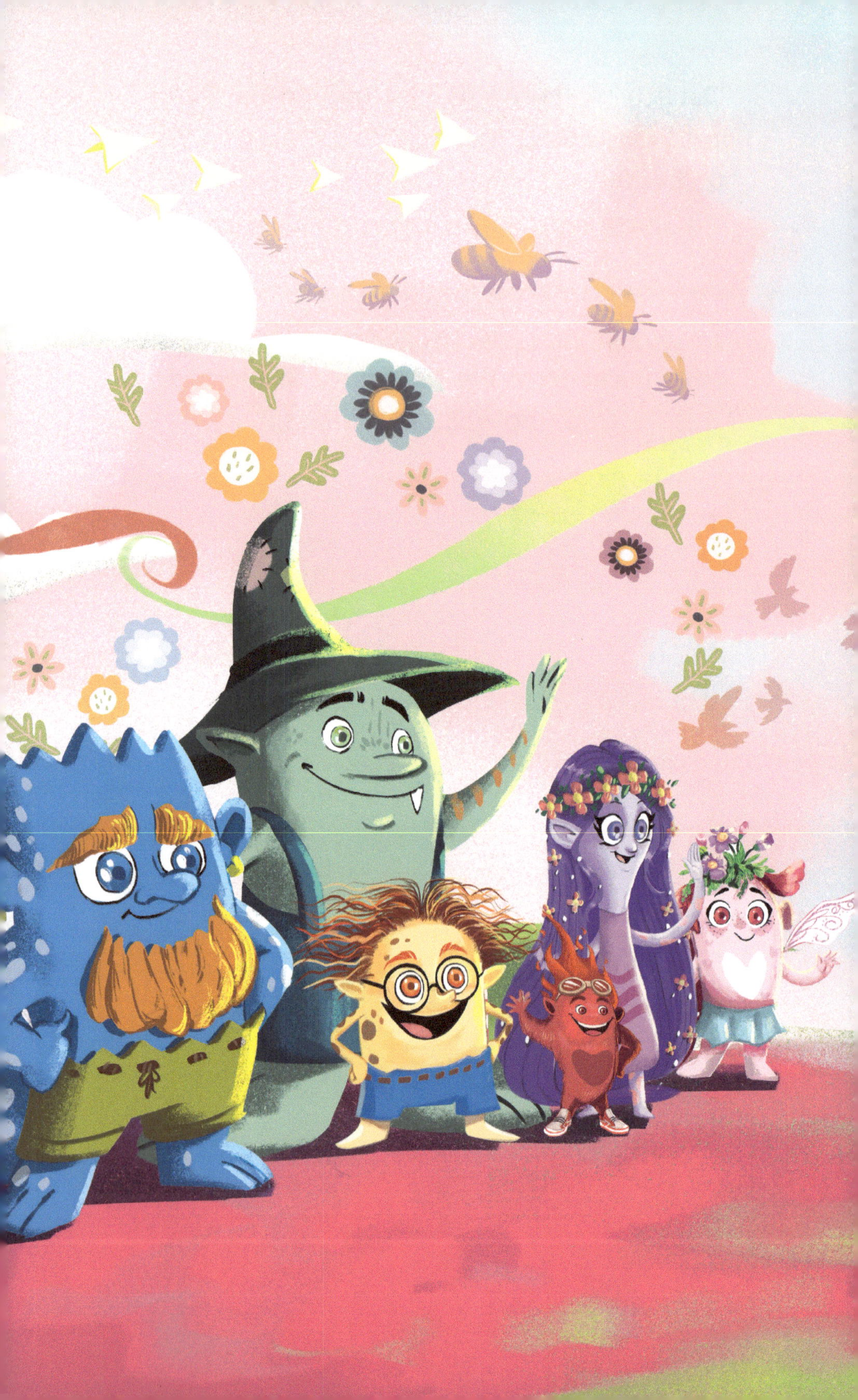

Bobby walked towards the six trolls, opening his arms as wide as he could, and embraced them all together as tightly as he could.

"Thank you for being here," Bobby whispered. "We are always with you, no matter what happens. Now it's time for you to go. Someone is waiting for you," said Rosy, the pink troll of gratitude.

Bobby grinned, waved at everyone again, and headed toward Kaya's house. He couldn't wait to see his friend and apologize to her. As soon as he spotted her cottage, he began to shout, "KAAAAAYAAAAA, KAAAAAAYAAAA!"

Kaya appeared at the door, surprised by the commotion and wondering who was making such a noise. Then she saw Bobby running towards her, waving his arms and smiling.

"Kaya! I'm sorry," Bobby said as soon as he reached her. "I behaved very badly, and I shouldn't have. I got angry because you didn't want to play tag. But we could have made a deal. Hide-and-seek first, then tag," Bobby said in one breath. "I promise that if I get angry next time, I won't shout or push. I'll respect your wishes too and listen better!"

Kaya didn't say anything; she simply hugged her dear friend.

"I forgive you, Bobby," Kaya said. "I shouldn't have gotten angry either. We could have played tag first. I'm sorry too. And what I said... I didn't mean it!"
"I forgive you, too," Bobby quickly replied. "Would you like to play?"
"Yes. How about riding our bikes?" Kaya suggested.
"Great idea!" Bobby replied, and they headed towards Bobby's house together to pick up his bike.

The most beautiful Rainbow appeared in the sky above the two friends as they walked along the road.

For a moment, the six trolls of the Magic Rainbow showed themselves before the Rainbow disappeared, just in time to hear the most beautiful words between the two friends:

"Thank you for being my friend."

Note to the Parent

Thank you for your trust. I hope this book has been helpful to you. I am Sety H, a certified specialist and consultant in positive parenting. If you would like to learn more about its methods, you may download for free my parenting course via the mobile app "Ommm positive parenting".

I hope that together we can rediscover the beauty of parenting in our everyday life. And add a little bit of magic too.

About The Author

Sety H., is a wife, a mother of two boys, a certified positive parenting coach, a linguist, and a quality expert. But most of all is a person with a big compassionate heart that is following her dream of making the world a better place. That dream took roots in her mind during her rough childhood in Bulgaria. Since then she has travelled the world, lived, studied and worked in the US, South Korea, the UK and finally settled down in the Netherlands. In all her travels she kept searching for a way to fulfil that little girl's dream.

Her career progression did not succeed in giving her that answer for a long time. Until the day she became a mother and the Universe opened up a new horizon to her. It was then, in 2015, that she found the power of positive parenting and felt the immediate click. It all made sense to her and showed her a clear way of bringing her "happy" in the everyday life. It was also then that she started to write. Her first book was published only a year later, after her son's first birthday. She was on her journey and started to realize the power that parenting brought. The power to make the world a better place. By raising children with love, compassion, kindness and respect she could ensure that flicker of hope. Through her stories and books she started communicating with hundreds of parents, bringing them laughter and comfort in the most challenging times of parenthood. Her first 4 books were written and published only in Bulgaria.

When her second boy was born in the midst of the first lockdown in 2020 everything came into place and Sety finally understood what needed to be done. She signed up for a parenting course, then another and another and got certified as a positive parenting coach. Not long after, in 2021, she published her very own parenting course that was built into a mobile application - Ommm positive parenting. The app is available in three languages (Bulgarian, English and Dutch) and is also the first positive parenting course-app in Bulgarian. With this she could reach thousands of parents worldwide, extending a helping, guiding hand to those who wanted to raise their families with those same values. And this was the only way we could ensure that better world she had always dreamt of.

In 2023, inspired by her two boys, she wrote the children's book series "Bobby's tales of life and wonder", believing her words could bring joy, guidance and magic to both children and parents.

Bobby's Tales
Of Life and Wonder

More titles coming to the series:

Mommy always comes back
Bobby and the Circle of Friends
Bobby and the Road of Smiles
Bobby and the Upside-Down World of Dreams
Bobby and the Magic of Animals
Bobby and the Jar of Stars
Bobby and the Soul Firefly

Milton Keynes UK
Ingram Content Group UK Ltd.
UKHW050313130224
437742UK00001B/9